I WANT TO BE AN

ASTRONAUT

Written by
Jonathan Reule

Illustration
Phan Quỳnh Trang

Storyboard
Christiane Tee

First paperback edition May 2023
ISBN 978-981-17320-9-6

Published by Unibino Pte. Ltd.
31 Rochester Drive Level 3, #03-47 Singapore 138637

www.unibino.com

Have you ever looked up at the night sky and wondered what's out there beyond our world? Well, if that's the case, then you're not alone. People have been wondering for thousands of years what mysteries the heavens might hold for us. In ancient times, various theories, myths, and wild speculations abounded about the stars and planets. But despite our long-standing curiosity, we still have much to learn about the universe and its hidden mysteries.

While the modern world has seen many technological advancements, our exploration of the vast unknown remains limited. However, the desire to venture into space continues to capture the imagination of many, whether it's experiencing weightlessness or conducting experiments in new atmospheres. So if you feel brave enough to take on such an adventure into outer space, then perhaps becoming an astronaut may be the perfect career for you.

But where did this dream first start? How did we get to the point where we were able to send men and women into the Earth's orbit? Well, the answer takes us back many thousands of years, long before we had the various technological gadgets we have today. You see, from the very first time we gazed up into the night skies and realised there was something greater than ourselves up there, we had a dream to one day touch that realm.

Of course, it's difficult for us to know for sure how ancient humans perceived the sun, moon, and stars. Yet, when we look at evidence from cave paintings and other carved statues, we can make an educated guess as to what they were thinking. Based on what we've seen, it seems likely that they viewed these celestial bodies as divine beings whom they wanted to emulate.

These beliefs endured for ages, with many cultures holding the notion that ethereal beings resided in the skies, shining down upon us during the night. Some believed that the stars were the spirits of their ancestors, while others believed that these celestial bodies had control over their lives on Earth.

Interestingly, there are many stories from ancient texts about humans attempting to reach the heavens. One such story is the Tower of Babel, where a civilisation tried to reach their god in the sky by building a giant tower. However, the story ends with the tower collapsing and the people growing too confused to communicate with one another anymore. While this story is likely just a myth, it speaks to the longstanding human fascination with the possibility of reaching beyond our earthly bounds.

Continuing our exploration of ancient beliefs about space travel, we see a common theme emerge across many cultures. For instance, some believed that comets were gods travelling around in spaceships, while others saw them as messages from the gods, warning of impending disasters on Earth.

In addition, gods were often associated with the sky, riding chariots or floating on clouds. In the ancient Vedic religion, we see this quite clearly with the Pushpaka Viman, which is often depicted as a flying sky chariot with two giant birds as its steeds.

For quite some time, these gods were untouchable beings to us. The thought of reaching the heavens by artificial means soon became taboo. We limited ourselves to keeping our feet firmly planted on the ground, believing that the world above us was sacred and out of our reach.

Although the idea of exploring the unknown in space captivated the human imagination, throughout history, there have been many warnings about the dangers of reaching the stars. One famous example is the tale of Icarus, who fashioned wings for himself and flew too close to the sun, causing the glue to melt and sending him plummeting back to Earth.

Such cautionary tales reinforced the notion that it was better to stay grounded and avoid the perils of the heavens.

Even if we didn't take conscious steps towards space travel during certain periods of our history, there were other inventions that helped build the foundation for future space exploration. During the middle ages during the Song Dynasty in China, the very first rockets were created in an attempt to thwart Mongolian armies. These initial rockets were used during war times to not only scare the enemy but also potentially injure the opposing soldiers.

After the war, rockets evolved, taking on new functions and uses that weren't solely geared towards violence. Soon, imperial China started to use these rockets as a form of entertainment by filling them with different types of gunpowder and launching them into the skies. This is how fireworks were invented and eventually helped to inspire the design of modern-day rocket boosters.

Over the next few centuries, though, rockets became less common, as many found them to be impractical during times of war. It wasn't until the 1700s, during the Anglo-Mysorean War, that these rockets saw a resurgence in usage. At this time, the Indian army devised a metal-cased rocket that they used to fire on the British army.

The Mysorean rockets proved to be highly effective against the British armies, to the point that the British attempted to salvage the remaining rockets to recreate them for their own arsenals. As a result, a heavier version of the wartime rocket, known as the Congreve rocket, was developed to inflict more damage on enemy armies.

Unfortunately, despite the devastating effects of rockets and bombs in wars and conflicts around the world, we continued to develop and deploy them. This led us to the Cold War era after World War II, where the United States and the Soviet Union engaged in a tense standoff, with both sides threatening to launch highly destructive bombs that could have resulted in the annihilation of all life on Earth.

For many, this was a very scary time, where most felt the world might end at any moment. But while these countries were in a stalemate with one another, something else arose between them, a different type of competition. That's what led to the period known as the Space Race, where the US and Soviet Union both tried their best to send the first rocket up into space!

On October 4th, 1957, the Soviet Union achieved a historic milestone in human history by launching the first man-made satellite, Sputnik, into orbit. This achievement marked a major turning point in the Space Race. Soon after, the Soviet Union sent the first astronaut, Yuri Gagarin, into space. Gagarin successfully orbited the planet before returning back to Earth, cementing the Soviet Union's lead in the race to explore space.

This victory, of course, caused the US to double down on their efforts so they weren't left behind in this space race by pledging to send a man to the moon by the end of the decade. This feat was finally accomplished in July of 1969 when the US landed the Apollo crew on the moon, where they took some small steps for themselves and a giant leap for mankind.

Since then, space travel has become more prominent, with several countries sending rockets out past the mesosphere. We've even gone so far as to send robots onto different planets, such as Venus and Mars. Although we've yet to send astronauts to those planets, there are many working tirelessly to make that a reality within the next few decades. For now, the most popular place you'll find astronauts travelling to is the international space station.

This satellite was launched into orbit in 1998 and has become a great symbol of how far we've come as a society. You see, the ISS was not simply created by one nation but by many nations. It demonstrates what we can achieve when we put our differences aside and learn to work together, and that's just what those Cold War rivals did when they built this station alongside each other.

Being an astronaut is not for the faint of heart. Firstly, most astronauts are well-trained in their respective fields, from engineering, astrophysics, space piloting, and plenty of other rigorous scientific disciplines. Secondly, astronauts need to be in great physical shape, as travelling into space and living there for some time takes a big toll on their bodies.

Thirdly, astronauts have to be prepared to spend time away from their families and friends while on missions. Even though they might be able to watch the Earth from outside their windows, that doesn't mean they'll be close to the people they love.

Lastly, astronauts need to be brave before going into space. Sometimes their job might require them to gear up in a spacesuit and go outside the ISS to fix parts or perform other regular maintenance checks. In order to do that properly, they'll need to keep their cool and focus on their task at hand, not the fact that they're in outer space, miles above the Earth.

But what do astronauts do up in space, and why are they so important? Many conduct experiments in the zero-gravity environment, where they can test their hypothesis under ideal conditions offered in the ISS. Others may travel into space to help plan for future projects, such as looking into creating a lunar base where humans may one day live on the Moon!

It's also good to note what astronauts do when they aren't up in space. Most will be helping other astronauts prepare for upcoming missions. This may come in the form of helping new astronauts prepare for the intense blastoff experience during flight, or they might give some feedback on proposed projects intended for the mission's duration. They can also be found in the mission control centre, keeping in communication with the astronauts floating miles above the Earth.

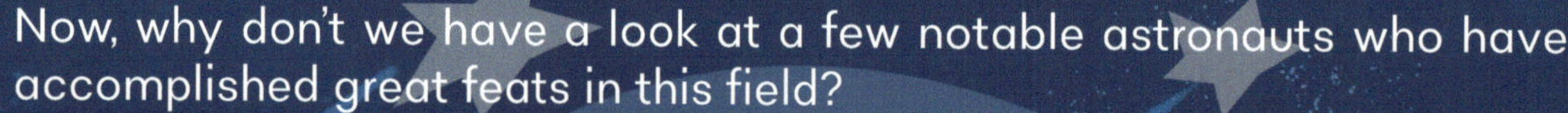

Now, why don't we have a look at a few notable astronauts who have accomplished great feats in this field?

Laika, the first animal to successfully orbit the Earth, is a famous example. According to some records, Laika was a stray dog who was found on the streets of Moscow and adopted by the Soviet Union's space program as an honorary astronaut. Sadly, she overheated during the flight and passed away before being brought back to Earth. Despite this tragedy, she remains a hero to many space enthusiasts as one of the bravest animals to venture up into the firmament.

While Yuri Gagarin made history as the first human to travel into outer space, his successful flight and return to Earth also made him an instant celebrity. Despite his desire to join more space missions, he was soon banned by the Soviet Union, who feared the potential risks to their international celebrity. They couldn't take any chances that something might happen to him!

After Yuri Gagarin's historic flight into outer space, the race to explore the final frontier continued to captivate the world's attention. The most notable achievement in this race was the first manned mission to the Moon, which occurred on July 20, 1969. This mission, led by Buzz Aldrin, Neil Armstrong, and Michael Collins, was the culmination of years of planning, research, and hard work by thousands of scientists, engineers, and support staff at NASA.

However, the Soviet Union continued to lead the space race with another historic achievement. On June 16, 1963, Valentina Tereshkova, a Soviet cosmonaut, made history by becoming the first woman to travel to space. Tereshkova's mission demonstrated the Soviet Union's technological prowess and was a significant propaganda victory in the midst of the Cold War with the United States.

Space exploration has had a profound impact on society, both in terms of scientific advancements and cultural influence. From the invention of new technologies such as satellite communications and GPS to the way we think about our place in the universe - space exploration has touched almost every aspect of our lives.

As impressive as the history of space exploration has been, the future is even more promising. The importance of astronauts in our modern world lies in the fact that they help turn dreams into realities. With so much still to discover and explore, there will always be a need for brave men and women to take on the challenges of space exploration.

Who knows, maybe one day you too will be among the select few who fly high above the Earth or embark on a speedy rocket journey to Mars or beyond. The possibilities are endless, and the future of space exploration is boundless.

Shubhi Saxena
Founder, Unibino

My Inspiration

As a parent in this ever-changing world, it can sometimes feel overwhelming when it comes to our children's futures. New technologies seem to be arising almost every day, and with so many innovations, it creates unique professions which many of us wouldn't have dreamed to be necessary only a few years ago. Which to me is a good thing. Because with so much variety, my children can have the opportunity to pick a career that will fit their personalities and build upon their strengths. As you may imagine, this desire within me to provide my children with the resources they needed to thrive, led me to search out books that would be easy enough for them to understand while teaching them about various professions.

Only, I found that these books were few and far between. Even if I could find a book about a certain profession geared towards young readers, I found them sparse inside and limited to only certain careers that may not fit my children's abilities. This is when I came up with the idea to write my own children's books, teaching them about all the various careers in the modern world. After months of researching different professions and learning more than I ever expected, I quickly realised this was going to be a bigger project than I first anticipated. I dove into the histories of these professions, discovering links to the past, and why these professions were now so important.

Ultimately my goal was to offer my children options, to show them that there is no one set path for everyone. But in this, I stumbled upon something bigger. I wanted to share this with future generations. To share with all children and parents about these careers, to help spark curiosity, and to instil a passion for the future. Everyone has special talents and abilities, and I hope that this series will be able to offer clarity and inspiration to children around the world. Because at the end of the day, it's never too early to start dreaming and never too late to take action. With this, I hope you enjoy this series and that your young ones become the best versions of themselves as they can achieve.

www.ingramcontent.com/pod-product-compliance
Ingram Content Group UK Ltd.
Pitfield, Milton Keynes, MK11 3LW, UK
UKHW060102300726
14090UKWH00003B/347

* 9 7 8 9 8 1 1 7 3 2 0 9 6 *